DAVID BEDNALL
MAKE WE MERRY

SSAA and organ (with optional brass)

Contents

Duration: 25 minutes

An accompaniment for brass ensemble, organ, and percussion is available on hire/rental from the publisher or appropriate agent. For performances with brass, the organ part available on hire/rental should be used, rather than the part in the vocal score.

MUSIC DEPARTMENT

OXFORD
UNIVERSITY PRESS

for Edward Whiting and Benenden Chapel Choir
and with grateful thanks to Julian Metherell for his kind and generous support

Make We Merry

DAVID BEDNALL

1. Make we merry

Anon. c.1500

For now is the time, now is the time, now is the time of Chri - ste - mas!

Let no man_ come in - to this hall, Nor

groom, nor page, nor yet mar - shall, But that some sport he bring with all. Make_ we mer-ry both

more and less, For now is the time, now is the time,

now is the time of Chri - ste - mas!

If he say that_ he can - not sing, Some o - ther sport then let him_ bring, That it may please at this feast - ing.

Make_ we mer-ry, make_ we mer-ry, make_ we mer-ry, both more and less.

If he say naught can_ he do, Then,

Clifton Village, 11 January 2018

2. The time draws near

Alfred, Lord Tennyson (1809–92)

Four voi - ces— of four ham - lets round, From far— and near, on mead and moor,

Man.

Swell———out and fail, as if a door Were shut be-tween me and the sound.

Swell———out and fail, as if a door Were shut be-tween me and the sound.

Gt.

Each voice— four

Each voice— four

Gt.

chan-ges on the wind, That now___ di-late,___ and now___ de-crease,

Peace and good-will,___ good-will and peace, Peace and good-will to all man-kind.

Peace and good-will,___ good-will and peace,___ Peace and good-will to all man-kind.

S./A.

This

Clifton Village, 19 January 2018

3. The Christ-child lay on Mary's lap

G. K. Chesterton (1874–1936)

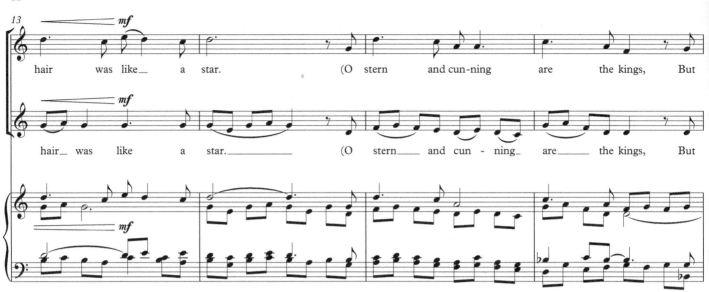

wea - ry, wea - ry is the world, But here the world's de - sire.) The

wea - ry, wea - ry is the world, But here the world's de - sire.) The

Christ - child stood at Ma - ry's knee, His hair was like a crown, And

Christ - child stood at Ma - ry's knee, His hair was like a crown, And

all the flowers looked up at him, And all the stars looked down.

all the flowers looked up at him, And all the stars looked down.

Ped.

Clifton Village, 20 January 2018

4. All this night shrill chanticleer

William Austin (1587–1634)

night_____ Hea - ven and ev - 'ry twink-ling light,___ All____ a - maz - ing,

night_____ Hea - ven and ev - 'ry twink-ling light,___ All____ a - maz - ing,

Still_____ stand gaz - ing, An - gels, pow - ers and_ all____ that be,

Still_____ stand gaz - ing, An - gels, pow - ers and_ all_____ that be,

Wake and joy___ this Sun, this Sun to see.

Wake_ and joy___ this Sun,___ this Sun___ to see.

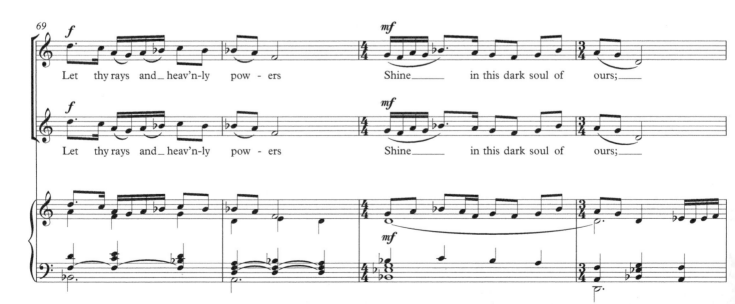

Clifton Village, 21 January 2018

5. *Moonless darkness stands between*

Gerard Manley Hopkins (1844–99)

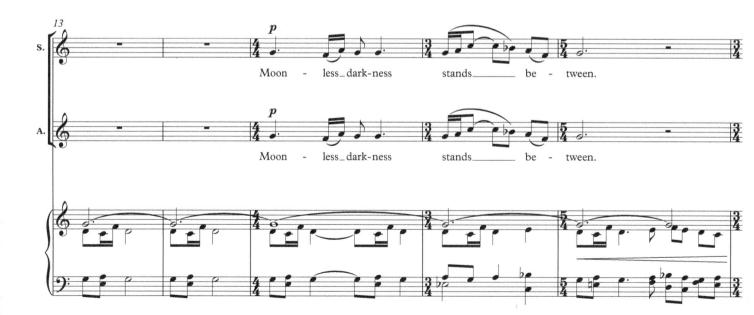

Moon - less dark-ness stands be - tween.

Moon - less dark-ness stands be - tween.

and_____ al - way:_____ Now_____ be - gin on Christ - mas day.

and_____ al - way:_____ Now_____ be - gin on Christ - mas day.

Moon - less_dark-ness stands_____ be - tween.

Moon - less_dark-ness stands_____ be - tween.

Man.

Past, the past,_____ no more be seen!_____

Past,_____ the_ past,_ no more be seen!_____

Ped.

Clifton Village, 31 March 2018

6. Sweet was the song

from William Ballet's Lute Book (16th cent.)

* pronounce as *loo-la*

she to Beth - lem Ju-da came And was de-li-vered of a Son That bless - ed Je-sus hath to

name. Lul - la, lul - la, lul - la, lul-la-by, lul - la, lul-la-by. 'Sweet babe,' quoth

name. Lul - la, lul - la, lul - la, lul-la-by, lul - la, lul-la-by. 'Sweet

she, And rocked him sweet-ly on her knee.

babe,' quoth she, And rocked him sweet-ly on her knee.

7. Let others look for pearl and gold

Robert Herrick (1591–1674)

* May be used in performance if necessary
† *tabbies* = silk taffetas

* *clout* = cloth

gold,_____ for pearl and gold, Tis-sues, or tab - bies ma-ni - fold:

gold,_____ for_ pearl and gold, Tis - sues, or_ tab-bies ma - ni - fold:

gold,_____ for pearl and gold, Tis - sues, or tab - bies ma - ni-fold:

gold,_____ for pearl and gold, Tis - sues, or_ tab-bies ma - ni-fold:

One on - ly lock of that sweet hay Where-on the bless - ed ba - by lay,

One_ on - ly lock of that sweet hay Where-on the bless - ed, the bless - ed ba - by_ lay,

One on - ly lock of that sweet hay Where-on the bless - ed, the bless - ed_ ba - by lay,

One_ on - ly lock of that sweet hay Where-on the bless - ed, bless - ed_ ba - by lay,

Clifton Village, 31 March 2018

8. Make we joy now

Anon 15th cent.

¹ In which Christ is born

32

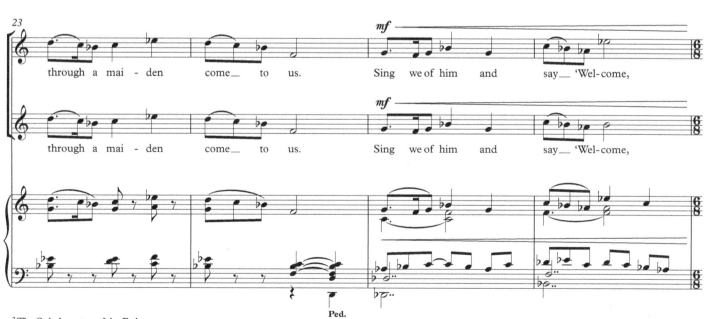

f

Ve - ni Re-demp-tor, ve - ni Re-demp-tor, ve - ni Re-demp-tor gen - ci - um.' [3]

f

Ve - ni Re-demp-tor, ve - ni Re-demp-tor, ve - ni Re-demp-tor gen - ci - um.' [3]

f

31

Make_ we joy now in_ this fest In_ quo Chris - tus na - tus est.

Make_ we joy now in_ this fest In_ quo Chris - tus na - tus est.

mf legato

Man.

Ped.

35

mf —————————————————————————————————— *ff*

E - ya, e - ya, e - ya, e - ya!

mf —————————————————————————————————— *ff*

E - ya, e - ya, e - ya, e - ya!

f

Man.

[3] Come, Redeemer of the nations

⁴ Let every age perceive (that)

ver - bum su - per - num pro - di - ens. [5]

ver - bum su - per - num pro - di - ens. [5]

E - ya, e - ya, e - ya, e - ya!

E - ya, e - ya, e - ya, e - ya!

A so - lis or - tus car - di - ne [6] So might - y a lord is

A so - lis or - tus car - di - ne [6] So might - y a lord is

[5] The high Word forthcoming   [6] From the rising of the sun

7 Which our father Adam defiled

10 O Light of the Holy Trinity

11 Glory to thee, O Lord!

40

Music originated by Andrew Jones
Printed in England by Halstan & Co. Ltd, Amersham, Bucks.

Clifton Village, 4 April 2018